Introduction

Date: 4/14/14

I was sitting back this past Sunday, not realizing that it was Palm Sunday. I got out of bed and it was after 10AM. All of a suddenly, I was inspired to write a book of poetry about the resurrection and about The Lord Jesus Christ. As I walked in town, I could feel the presence of The Lord. As I sat down on the park bench in downtown Wilmington, I started writing. The poems just started flowing from me, giving praises to The Lord and just worshiping him in poetry. I finished writing my last poem Monday morning and I feel so Blessed! This is my way to give my thanks and praise to my Lord and Savior Jesus Christ. Included is a list of 44 Prophecies Jesus Fulfilled. There are over 300 prophecies that Jesus fulfilled. Showing that he is The Son of God. Also included are **some verses related to** *I Am the Resurrection* **from the King James Version of The Bible. I hope this book is a blessing to everyone that reads it and brings you closer to Christ. And remember, Jesus loves you and so do I!**

God Bless,

Charles Johnson AKA The Homeless Poet

They scorned him

They scorned him
They gave him a crown of thorns
They mocked him
They sentenced him to death

They made him carry
The cross of his death
As his blood flowed
His body, wracked with pain

They hung him on the cross
As blood poured from his wounds
His pain unbearable
His suffering great

He took upon him
The sins of the world
He became so much like us
That even his Father turned away from him.

Yes he loved us that much
Why don't we love him?

Who can deny

Who can deny
The love of God
When he turned over his son
To sinful man

What greater love is there
To allow his son
To hang on the cross
With the sins of the world

He could've destroyed us all
Been finished with us He
could've started over
But he did not

He sent his son
His only son
To set us free
To give us life

Life abundantly

My praises are to you

My praises are to you
My Lord For
only you
Died for me

Who else can make that claim?
Who else can make that statement?
Who else can give eternal life?

Only you My Lord
To only you Lord will I bow
To only you Lord will I pray
To only you Lord will I serve

Only you Lord Rose
from the grave And
defeated death

Life is in you My Lord You
are worthy of all praise You
are life
You are salvation
You are Lord

The blood he shed

The blood he shed
On the cross Was
the blood
We should've shed

The pain he endured While
hanging on the cross Was
the pain
We should've endured

The crown of thorns
That was put through his skin
Was the thorns
That should've pierced our skin

But yet the nails through
His feet and hands The
suffering
All that should've been us
But he said no
I love you enough
To bear it all for you

His love

His love is so strong
That not even death could hold him

His love is so strong
That the demons trembled before him

His love is so strong
That the grave couldn't hold him

His love is so strong
That Satan had to bow to him

And lastly

His love is so strong
That he died for us

He is the good shepherd

He is the good shepherd
He laid down his life for his sheep
He willingly went to die

He was not afraid
He could've said no I won't
But he didn't

Like a good shepherd
He protected his flock
From the gates of Hell

He would go there
To the darkness of Hell
So his sheep would not

In three days, he rose
He was the victor over Hell
He was the victor over death

All power was given to him
And every knee shall bow
To the name Jesus

G – Great
O – Outstanding
D – Deliverance

L – Love
S – Salvation
D – Deliverance

S – Saved
A – And
V – Victories
E – Evangelism
D – Delivered

With you Lord

With you Lord
I can climb a mountain
I can withstand any storm
I can win any battle

With you Lord
I can walk through trouble
I can walk upright
I can walk in Love

With you Lord
I can face the world
I can face my fears
I can face my life

With you Lord
I know I'm free
I know I'm saved
I know I'm loved

With you my Lord

You don't have, To fight alone

You don't have
To fight alone
The battle is not yours
It's the Lord's

He will fight your battles
He will protect you from harm
He will keep you safe

He will ease your pain
He will wipe your tears
If you just call on him

He will give you peace That
passes all understanding If
you just believe in him

He hears the cries of his children
He sees the tears of his children
He will answer their prayers
If you let him

He went to the cross

He went to the cross
For you and me
The shedding of his blood
Set us free

They hung him
On the cross Now
he has power To
set us free

He went to the cross
For you and me

My life was a wreck
I couldn't get no rest
Time and time again
I fell deeper in sin

I looked to the cross
To save me 'cause I'm lost

He went to the cross
For you and me

He looked down at me
My child, be set free
He shed blood, let me know
That he loved me so

I looked at the cross

To save me 'cause I'm lost

He went to the cross
For you and me

For you and me
For you and me He
went to the cross
For you and me

Beautiful Jesus

Beautiful Jesus
Beautiful blood
Flowing all over me
All from his love

Cleansing my body
Cleansing my soul
Flowing all through me
Cleans and makes me as gold

Beautiful Jesus
Glory divine
Flowing in glory
Sweeter than wine

Because of your mercy
Now can see My
eyes are open I
see victory

I will serve you
All of my days
'Til when you come
And take me away

C – Christians
R – Redeemed
O – Overcoming
S – Sin
S – Salvation

Freed by the blood

Freed by the blood That
was shed at the cross
Freed by the blood
Salvation for the lost

Because of the blood
I've been set free
Because of the blood
I have victory

Freed by the blood
That was shed at the cross

I was in despair
I nobody cared
I felt all alone
I didn't have a home

Then Jesus came to me
Set my spirit free
Now I have the victory

The books of the <u>Old Testament</u> contain many passages about the Messiah—all prophecies <u>Jesus Christ</u> fulfilled. For instance, <u>the crucifixion of Jesus</u> was foretold in <u>Psalm 22:16-18</u> approximately 1,000 years before Christ was born, long before this method of execution was even practiced.

Some Bible scholars suggest there are more than 300 prophetic Scriptures <u>completed</u> in the <u>life</u> of Jesus.

Although this list is not exhaustive, you'll find 44 messianic predictions clearly fulfilled in Jesus Christ, along with supporting references from the Old and New Testament.

Prophecies Jesus Fulfilled

44 Prophecies Jesus Christ Fulfilled			
	Prophecies About Jesus	*Old Testament Scripture*	*New Testament Fulfillment*
1	*Messiah would be born of a woman.*	*Genesis 3:15*	*Matthew 1:20* *Galatians 4:4*
2	*Messiah would be born in <u>Bethlehem</u>.*	*Micah 5:2*	*Matthew 2:1* *Luke 2:4-6*
3	*Messiah would be born of a virgin.*	*Isaiah 7:14*	*M tthew 1:22-23* *L ke 1:26-31*
4	*Messiah would come from the line of <u>Abraham</u>.*	*Genesis 12:3* *Genesis 22:18*	*Matthew 1:1* *Romans 9:5*
5	*Messiah would be a descendant of <u>Isaac</u>.*	*Genesis 17:19* *Genesis 21:12*	*Luke 3:34*
6	*Messiah would be a descendant of <u>Jacob</u>.*	*Numbers 24:17*	*Matthew 1:2*
7	*Messiah would come from the*	*Genesis 49:10*	*Luke 3:33*

	tribe of Judah.		Hebrews 7:14
8	Messiah would be heir to King David's throne.	2 Samuel 7:12-13 Isaiah 9:7	Luke 1:32-33 Romans 1:3
9	Messiah's throne will be anointed and eternal.	Psalm 45:6-7 Daniel 2:44	Luke 1:33 Hebrews 1:8-12
10	Messiah would be called Immanuel.	Isaiah 7:14	Matthew 1:23
11	Messiah would spend a season in Egypt.	Hosea 11:1	Matthew 2:14-15
12	A massacre of children would happen at Messiah's birthplace.	Jeremiah 31:15	Matthew 2:16-18
13	A messenger would prepare the way for Messiah	Isaiah 40:3-5	Luke 3:3-6
14	Messiah would be rejected by his own people.	Psalm 69:8 Isaiah 53:3	John 1:11 John 7:5
15	Messiah would be a prophet.	Deuteronomy 18:15	Acts 3:20-22
16	Messiah would be preceded by Elijah.	Malachi 4:5-6	Matthew 11:13-14
17	Messiah would be declared the Son of God.	Psalm 2:7	Matthew 3:16-17
18	Messiah would be called a Nazarene.	Isaiah 11:1	Matthew 2:23
19	Messiah would bring light to Galilee.	Isaiah 9:1-2	Matthew 4:13-16
20	Messiah would speak in parables.	Psalm 78:2-4 Isaiah 6:9-10	Matthew 13:10-15, 34-35
21	Messiah would be sent to heal the brokenhearted.	Isaiah 61:1-2	Luke 4:18-19
22	Messiah would be a priest	Psalm 110:4	Hebrews 5:5-6

	after the order of <u>Melchizedek</u>.		
23	Messiah would be called King.	Psalm 2:6 Zechariah 9:9	Matthew 27:37 Mark 11:7-11
24	Messiah would be praised by <u>little children</u>.	Psalm 8:2	Matthew 21:16
25	Messiah would be betrayed.	Psalm 41:9 Zechariah 11:12-13	Luke 22:47-48 Matthew 26:14-16
26	Messiah's price money would be used to buy a potter's field.	Zechariah 11:12-13	Matthew 27:9-10
27	Messiah would be falsely accused.	Psalm 35:11	Mark 14:57-58
28	Messiah would be silent before his accusers.	Isaiah 53:7	Mark 15:4-5
29	Messiah would be spat upon and struck.	Isaiah 50:6	Matthew 26:67
30	Messiah would be hated without cause.	Psalm 35:19 Psalm 69:4	John 15:24-25
31	Messiah would be <u>crucified</u> with criminals.	Isaiah 53:12	Matthew 27:38 Mark 15:27-28
32	Messiah would be given vinegar to drink.	Psalm 69:21	Matthew 27:34 John 19:28-30
33	Messiah's hands and feet would be pierced.	Psalm 22:16 Zechariah 12:10	John 20:25-27
34	Messiah would be mocked and ridiculed.	Psalm 22:7-8	Luke 23:35
35	Soldiers would gamble for Messiah's garments.	Psalm 22:18	Luke 23:34 Matthew 27:35-36
36	Messiah's bones would not be broken.	Exodus 12:46 Psalm 34:20	John 19:33-36

37	Messiah would be forsaken by God.	Psalm 22:1	Matthew 27:46
38	Messiah would pray for his enemies.	Psalm 109:4	Luke 23:34
39	Soldiers would pierce Messiah's side.	Zechariah 12:10	John 19:34
40	Messiah would be buried with the rich.	Isaiah 53:9	Matthew 27:57-60
41	Messiah would resurrect from the dead.	Psalm 16:10 Psalm 49:15	Matthew 28:2-7 Acts 2:22-32
42	Messiah would ascend to heaven.	Psalm 24:7-10	Mark 16:19 Luke 24:51
43	Messiah would be seated at God's right hand.	Psalm 68:18 Psalm 110:1	Mark 16:19 Matthew 22:44
44	Messiah would be a sacrifice for sin.	Isaiah 53:5-12	Romans 5:6-8

Some Bible verses related to *I Am the Resurrection* **from the King James Version**

John 11:25 - Jesus said unto her, I am the resurrection, and the life: he that believeth in me, though he were dead, yet shall he live:

John 14:6 - Jesus saith unto him, I am the way, the truth, and the life: no man cometh unto the Father, but by me.

John 11:25-26 - Jesus said unto her, I am the resurrection, and the life: he that believeth in me, though he were dead, yet shall he live: (Read More...)

John 5:28 - Marvel not at this: for the hour is coming, in the which all that are in the graves shall hear his voice,

John 17:3 - *And this is life eternal, that they might know thee the only true God, and Jesus Christ, whom thou hast sent.*

John 8:58 - *Jesus said unto them, Verily, verily, I say unto you, Before Abraham was, I am.*

John 5:24 - *Verily, verily, I say unto you, He that heareth my word, and believeth on him that sent me, hath everlasting life, and shall not come into condemnation; but is passed from death unto life.*

Revelation 1:18 - *I [am] he that liveth, and was dead; and, behold, I am alive for evermore, Amen; and have the keys of hell and of death.*

2 Peter 3:9 - *The Lord is not slack concerning his promise, as some men count slackness; but is longsuffering to us-ward, not willing that any should perish, but that all should come to repentance.*

Romans 6:23 - *For the wages of sin [is] death; but the gift of God [is] eternal life through Jesus Christ our Lord.*

It is finished...

Looking unto Jesus, the author
and finisher of our faith, who for
the joy that was set before Him

endured the cross,

despising the shame,
and has sat down at the right
hand of the throne of God.
Hebrews 12:2

How Jesus Endured the Pain of the Cross By J. Lee Grady

Nobody performed an autopsy on Jesus' mangled body after He was taken down from the cross. But doctors who have studied the Bible's description of His death say the pain would have been beyond excruciating. In fact, the word excruciating means "out of the cross." Jesus literally defined the worst pain anyone could feel.

His suffering began in Gethsemane, when God laid the sins of the world on His beloved Son. The intense stress caused what physicians call hematridrosis, a condition in which blood seeps out of sweat glands. After His arrest, Jesus was flogged so mercilessly that his skin was stripped off His back, exposing muscle and bone.

After being slapped, punched, crowned with thorns and beaten with reeds, He was covered with a red robe and led to Golgotha. There, Roman soldiers drove seven-inch nails into his wrists (most likely hitting the median nerve, causing more blinding pain) and then they rammed another nail into his feet.

At that point, doctors suggest, Jesus would have suffered dislocation of His shoulders, cramps and spasms, dehydration from severe blood loss, fluid in His lungs and eventual lung collapse and heart failure. Yet He refused to take a pain-killing solution (see Matt. 27:34). He chose to endure the pain for us.

So how did Jesus handle this agony? Many scholars believe He meditated on Psalm 22 throughout His ordeal. He would have already memorized the prophetic prayer—which is quoted more often in the New Testament than any other Old Testament passage. It describes in detail the death of the Messiah. Imagine Jesus muttering the words of this psalm as He gasped for breath:

"My God, My God, why have you forsaken me?" (Psalm 22:1, NASB). The gospels record Jesus praying this from the cross. Any Jew who heard it would have known He was quoting David's prayer.

"But I am a worm and not a man; a reproach of men, and despised by the people" (v. 6). Jesus said these words as a crowd of angry mockers insulted Him. Matthew Henry points out that worms were used in Bible times to dye red fabric. Jesus was stained red for us so that He could make our sins as white as snow.

"I am poured out like water, and all my bones are out of joint; my heart is like wax; it is melted within me" (v. 14). Some victims of Roman crucifixion took as long as nine days to die, but Jesus' death came in a matter of hours—probably because He had been flogged so cruelly before He was nailed to the rough wood.

"My strength is dried up like a potsherd, and my tongue cleaves to my jaws" (v. 15). Victims of crucifixion typically developed serious dehydration because of a lack of blood and oxygen.

"They pierced my hands and my feet. I can count all my bones. They look, they stare at me; they divide my garments among them, and for my clothing they cast lots" (v. 16b-18). Nowhere in the Old Testament is the cross described so clearly. Jesus' tormentors stripped Him of His clothes, and He bore our shame. We know from the Gospels that soldiers gambled for his tunic (see John 19:23-24).

But David's psalm does more than just predict the pain Jesus would experience. It ends in victory. Imagine Jesus muttering these words to Himself as He bled to death:

"I will tell of Your name to my brethren; in the midst of the assembly I will praise You" (v. 22). The author of Hebrews tells us that Jesus endured the Cross "because of the joy set before Him" (Heb. 12:2). Even as He hung in pitiful agony, He was thinking of union with His bride, the Church.

"All the ends of the world will remember and turn to the Lord, and all the families of the nations will worship before You. For the kingdom is the Lord's and He rules over the nations" (v. 28). Jesus died so that all nations might know His forgiveness and salvation! As He poured out His blood on that cross, He was thinking of China, India, Uganda, Bolivia, Cuba, Russia, Iceland, Iran, the United

States and every racial and ethnic group would one day know His love.

"They will come and will declare His righteousness to a people who will be born, that He has performed it" (v. 31). This closing verse in Psalm 22 speaks of the great and final victory of the Messiah. Interestingly, the original Hebrew in the last phrase ("He has performed it") can be translated, "It is finished." This is exactly what Jesus declared in John 19:30 as He breathed His last! Most likely He recited the entirety of Psalm 22 during the tedious process of death.

In our sophisticated culture, people don't like to talk about the barbaric treatment Jesus received, or about the fact that Jesus had to die to cleanse us from our sins. Let God give you a fresh revelation of the cross this week. And remember the words of the old hymn that says:

In the old rugged cross, stained with blood so divine,
A wondrous beauty I see;
For 'twas on that old cross Jesus suffered and died,
To pardon and sanctify me.

J. Lee Grady *is the former editor of* Charisma *and the director of The Mordecai Project* (themordecaiproject.org)*.

Made in the USA
Columbia, SC
22 December 2021

51059417R00015